Congratulations, Robbie.
I hope you find this as helpful
as I do.

Wishing you every blessing
for a fruitful ministry.

Bryan Stacey. 27.10.12.

Increase Our Faith

Father Tadeusz Dajczer

Increase
Our Faith

Meditations on the Eucharist

3

Eucharistic Renewal Books

Imprimatur
+ Rt. Rev. Christopher Budd
Bishop of Plymouth
United Kingdom, Devon, Plymouth
October 21, 2011

Original title: *Przymnóż nam wiary*

Translation and editorship by

Artur Polit
Reverend Bryan Storey

Scriptural excerpts are taken from the Revised Standard Version
of the Holy Bible, Catholic edition.

Published 2012
by
Eucharistic Renewal Books
1 Chy an Pronter
Bossiney Road
Tintagel, Cornwall
PL34 0AQ, UK
Phone/fax 01840 770663
e-mail: books@eucharisticrenewal.org
website: **eucharisticrenewal.org**

© Bolesław Szewc 2012

ISBN 978-0-9560798-3-1

Printed in Poland by Efekt s.j., ul. Lubelska 30/32,
00-802 Warszawa, www.nalubelskiej.pl

CONTENTS

Foreword by Archbishop Joseph Michalik
Metropolitan of Praemislia and Chairman of the
Polish Conference of Bishops vii

PART I 1
Eucharist, core of interior life 3
My 'yes' is my worship............................9
Eucharist, pathway to a new self................. 13

PART II 19
Concern for souls................................. 21
True love for the departed 25
Drama the world needs to discover 31

PART III 35
Every day prepares............................... 37
For God's glory?................................. 43
Eucharistic love gives birth to saints............. 47
Life as liturgy 53

PART IV 59
Tough challenge to find freedom................. 61
Emptiness God longs to fill...................... 67
Father, I adore You............................. 73
A woman of the Eucharist....................... 79

FOREWORD

BY

ARCHBISHOP JOSEPH MICHALIK

METROPOLITAN OF PRAEMISLIA AND CHAIRMAN OF THE POLISH CONFERENCE OF BISHOPS

'Increase our faith' is the third in the series of Father Professor Tadeusz Dajczer's books on the Eucharist. My conviction grows that the author could write more of these books; he could be writing them all the time since he is totally wrapped up in the Eucharist; he is fascinated and in love with It, quite unable not to talk about this great Love. It has been like this since the day Father Tadeusz discovered that God fell in love with us to the point of total

Eucharistic surrender in the living Mystery of the Resurrected Christ.

The plea contained in 'Increase our Faith' seems to be the really adequate response to that Mystery. Following Our Lord, the author teaches and seeks faith as life's most precious treasure. Maturity involves seeing God's action everywhere and experiencing His presence as more real than the world we normally know. Like the Apostles, we need to learn and ripen into more faith.

Father Tadeusz tells us that the best book on the Eucharist is the Eucharist Itself; It is the test of our faith just as it was for the people of Capharnaum. I do not believe enough; I do not pray enough. I do not ask for this great gift as I need to; faith 'touches' God insofar as I am humble in the spirit of Mary in the Cenacle. We need to remember that in the Cenacle it was Mary who taught the Apostles to persevere in faith by prayer.

'Magnificat' sums up Our Lady's spirituality; that summary uniquely helps us experience the Eucharistic mystery. She first accepted Jesus into Her body to become that extraordinary tabernacle; it is valuable to ask Her to extend Her maternal care for me, together with Jesus whom I receive in Holy Communion.

Faith is interrelated belief in the Mass and union with others. If I do not try to live by faith each day, I will lack faith during Mass the author warns. In this book, there are many similar warnings along with other deeply stimulating thoughts. Father Tadeusz tells us that not even for a moment is it worth living without God. The Eucharist helps us as It is the sacrament of love; It is an extraordinary sacrament of extraordinary love. I need to stay with Jesus in the tabernacle as long as it takes almost to feel His heartbeat. Here we may learn how to worship and find a different view of the world and its people. Through the Eucharist, without moving from where we are, everything becomes different. Thanks to the Mass, I become a contemporary of Jesus; through union with Him, I take part in a totally different reality. That reality primarily concerns God's glory and our salvation. Eucharistic experience allows Jesus to adore the Father in me. This prayer lets Him pray for the living and the dead, leading me to salvation. Thus He sanctifies the world and its people, teaching us to love; that means "looking outward together in the same direction", to create and accomplish joint goals.

The author laments living as if God does not exist, feeling no hunger for God. By this we will surely die unless we ourselves or someone else ask help for us. Our good fortune is that the entire Heavenly Host together with Our Lady, prays for our sanctification through surrendering to Christ Jesus.

We are grateful to Professor Dajczer for this new testimony of faith; he inspires us earnestly to follow the Eucharistic pathway; he helps us discover the beauty and richness of interior life; he leads us to find greater openness to this freedom; he underlines how Jesus sanctifies and loves within us and for us so that we can share in His worship of the Father. I have no doubt that this book will be received in gratitude by all who search for faith's healthy sustenance and enrichment.

+ *Józef Michalik*

+ Joseph Michalik

Part I

IN THE TEXT YOU WILL FIND THE AUTHOR OFTEN WRITES IN THE FIRST PERSON. HE DOES THIS NOT TO REVEAL HIS OWN INNER LIFE BUT TO AVOID TAKING UP THE ROLE OF TEACHER OR ADVISER.

EUCHARIST, CORE
OF INTERIOR LIFE

The Eucharist is the sacrament of faith[1]. Abraham reveals how faith needs to grow. It grew as he left Ur of the Chaldees; it grew enormously when God asked him to sacrifice his only son; it grew in all his anxious moments.

For Eucharistic renewal, I need to be alert within myself. Growing faith inspires ever deeper clinging to God. It is not just learning about God; increasing faith triggers hope. Abraham, "in hope he believed against hope" (cf. Rom 4:18) finds that by deeply clinging to God, love flourishes – *this is my God, He leads me.*

---

[1] Cf. *Catechism of the Catholic Church*, 1123.

His faith had the openness and meaning which are basic to interior life.

Interior life is faith, hope and love, developing from the humility necessary for receiving Eucharistic graces; this is His real redemptive, sanctifying work for us. Living faith, hope and love permit Eucharistic graces to transform my thoughts, feelings, will and memory. By grace, I begin new ways of thinking, feeling and desiring; God and my environment become quite different; I begin to see God in everything.

Interior life leads me to cling to Christ Jesus; I cling much more to the Eucharist; I become alive with Him; I move from 'celebrating something' to life with my Lord Jesus; I may even 'touch' God. The Eucharist received in faith, constantly enriches my path to ever maturing sanctity. Our Lord, through His Church, calls us to be saints. That necessarily involves interior insight. Other than true martyrdom, there is no other way.

Sanctity is interdependent interior life and Eucharist. As interior life grows, it naturally flourishes into good works. Grace is the life-blood of interior life without which our activity is egocentric. The primacy of interior life over action is unavoidable.

4

Pope John Paul II encourages us to deepen in prayer. Faith is the measure of prayer. Prayer causes God to transform us through powerful Eucharistic graces. This prayer is supremely to do with God's changing us rather than His changing His plans or giving us something. Prayer is good when our attitude improves in sorrow, belief and gratitude. It is best when we are unconscious of our improvement; when we are unconscious of it, it helps us towards greater humility, preventing our taking these graces for granted.

Deep prayer, rooted in humble faith, breaks up stubborn hearts. This "constantly reminds us of Christ's primacy and, in union with Him, the primacy of the interior life and of holiness"[2]. Accepting the primacy of grace over activity propels us towards God really present on the altar. As we grow in this, more grace takes root in us; we become more ready for unique Eucharistic personal sanctification.

If we do not pray, others will want us less and less. Pope John Paul 2nd speaks strongly about Our Lord's primacy; this has to involve the interior life of grace: "But it is fatal to forget that «without Christ we can

[2] John Paul II, *Novo millennio ineunte*, 38.

do nothing» (cf. Jn 15,5)"[3]. We are easily deceived by illusions; only prayer and Eucharistic life safely help us see through them.

God grants graces, trusting we will value them as our vital need. This is not theory; these strong words of Pope John Paul about the primacy of grace are uttered in full view of the source of Eucharistic redeeming sacramental graces. This is pivotal; He alone through this sacrament of redemption can radically transform us. We need this transformation through putting God first so that He, living in us, guides us to choose the true love and good which lasts instead of ceasing.

Five years after Pope John Paul's *Novo millennio ineunte*, his successor Pope Benedict returned to the subject of the primacy of grace by strongly reminding us of St. Bernard of Clairvaux's words concerning our vital need to pray and contemplate.[4]. Pope Benedict emphasises that this includes me and everybody else. I can easily get so absorbed in activity that I push out prayer and contemplation; this often causes my "hardness of heart" as St. Bernard calls it "suf-

[3] Ibid.

[4] The Sunday prayer, 20.08.2006. *L'Osservatore Romano*, 12/2006, p. 30.

fering of spirit, loss of understanding, dispersion of grace". Pope Benedict, through the words of a great saint who dares to admonish Pope Eugene III, tells us "See, where these accursed occupations can lead you, if you continue to lose yourself in them." [5]. The Pope, referring to St. Bernard, reminds us how much we need interior peace for an increase in faith; prayer and contemplation are what bring us to the wholesome sanity of sanctity.

Deep, trusting prayer needs to be the source of my activity, leading me to union with the One present in everything and everybody. He is present when I am kneeling before the tabernacle; He is there when I am open to Him; He is there as I try through faith to see the miracle beyond the altar. He transforms me, makes me whole, sanctifies me, loves me through and through; He does it all without any reservation.

Living the Eucharist means having Him central to my thoughts, desires and hopes; living the Eucharist and interior life are inextricably united; they are interdependent. Thanks to the Eucharist, I can come into immediate and objective contact with that once-for-all redemption, mysteriously taking

[5] Ibid.

place in the Mass. There is no interior life without redemption; all graces flow from the crucified and risen One. Redemption is now beyond time, eternal. The Eucharist reveals it; It can be touched by faith; It is our sacrament of redemption.

I need to approach our Eucharistic God in humility as He "opposes the proud, but gives grace to the humble." (1Pet 5,5). St. Therese of Avila helps by saying "what we must do is beg like the needy poor before a rich and great Emperor." [6].

I need to appreciate faith more. It is the unique way to infinite Love; it is the only immediate way to union with God; it is the appropriate way. [7]. Everything else is subordinate; faith leads to that healing wholeness inasmuch as I need it. We call it sanctity.

---

[6] *The Interior Castle*, IV, 3,5; Washington, D.C., 1980, volume two, p.329.

[7] Cf. St. John of the Cross, *The Ascent of Mount Carmel*, II, 9,1.

My 'yes' is my worship

The Eucharist is the sacrament of faith; It follows my faith and builds it up. God longs to share His vision with me. He wants to convince me of His caring rule present in the world.

He longs for me to share His vision and love. He wants me freed from my inadequate self-centredness so that I can share His life in the amazing fulfilment of divine care. Just like Jesus, the Father's will then becomes my sustaining force. (Jn 4,34).

The material world unconsciously worships God, always fulfilling His will. We men and women, on the other hand, are able to worship God consciously, yet unself-consciously. My everyday life can then be permeated with a prayer: *Yes, I want it because You want it; this is Your holy will.*

I frequently fail to understand His will. "If you understand him, He is not God" says Pope Benedict quoting St. Augustine.[8]. My life flourishes in the discovery of and living by God's frequently inscrutable ways. This is *life's liturgy*. Even if this sometimes seems overwhelmingly senseless, the more I grow into this *perpetual liturgy*, the more I shall find what I need. His love is unique. He paid the highest price for me; He died for me. It is only right that I should honour and worship Him with my 'yes'. If I concentrate more on asking for things, I need also to remember my vital need for prayer of praise which inherently feeds the Eucharistic Liturgy.

From time to time, I shall surely experience my powerlessness and unworthiness. Yet these are not obstacles; on the contrary, powerlessness and unworthiness open my heart to the incomprehensible mercy flowing from the Eucharist. He looks for poor, inept, even unworthy ones who through repentance, are flooded by grace.The Eucharist is thanksgiving to and worship of the Father. In every Mass we pray: *Blessed are you, Lord, God of all creation...* When I say 'blessed be God forever', I am sharing in that Old

[8] The encyclical *Deus caritas est*, 38.

Testament spirit of returning to Him what He gives to me. God blesses me; I repay in thanks and worship by underlining His greatness. With this praise I express my certainty; God will give me what I ask for. This is why I can adore Him even more.

The Old Testament is full of similar 'prayer blessings'. Tobit experienced difficulties; as he benefits from Omnipotence, he praises Him by thanksgiving and worship. (cf. Tob 13,2; 8,15-17; 11,14-17; 13,18). 'Thanksgiving worship' returned to God for His gifts, becomes Eucharistic; that is what Eucharist is. [9]."Faith is ... praise"; the Eucharist, sacrament of faith, is "sacrifice of praise". [10]. By making my activity worship of God, my life becomes Eucharistic. My final goal is to be eternal gift for Him, to open myself so much to the redemptive graces of the Eucharist that my whole life is for God's glory. So my life grows into more and more thanksgiving and praise.

I am to live for the Lord; our Church leads me to this meaningful goal; it points to the Eucharist as my

---

[9] Cf. the Eucharist as thanksgiving and praise: *Catechism of the Catholic Church*, 1358.

[10] *Catechism of the Catholic Church* , 2642, 2643.

Reality in every moment; each moment needs to be praise of God, to become Eucharistic.

Worthy art thou, our Lord and God, to receive today power and wealth and wisdom and might and honour and glory and blessing... (cf. Rev 5,9.12-13).

EUCHARIST, PATHWAY
TO A NEW SELF

We can give a variety of answers to the question 'why go to Mass?'. Perhaps I go out of duty; perhaps Sunday is unimaginable without Mass; perhaps I would feel bad if I missed; maybe it is part of my Sunday schedule. Various surveys ask 'What does Mass mean to you?'. It would be more to the point to ask what the Lord looks for in me. To say I go to be better or to join in the Church's life or emphasise the Lord's Day may sound all right; these replies might appeal to people. Yet would those answers appeal to Him?

The Lord God has it right. He expects a different answer. He would certainly expect us to say: *I go only so that You sanctify me, my God*. This is the answer He expects from me, because "the purpose of the sacraments is to sanctify men, to build up the Body of Christ and finally to give worship to God". [11].

The Eucharist is the way to that wholeness of sanctity; it is the sacrament which forms saints. It is the foundation of everything in that freely accepted meeting of grace and human will. The Eucharist opens me to ever present redeeming graces; I need a daily preparation before the Penitential Rite. My daily life needs to be true to that penitential Eucharistic preparation; I need to be ready for my interior transformation by Eucharistic graces. All my turbulences, falls and renewals are vital for my Eucharist. My struggles and openings to God's ceaseless actions are priceless assets. We prepare for Mass in daily events; these are where the fight for my sanctity takes place.

I'll learn more of my need to change to receive Holy Communion effectively because the Eucharist sanctifies my life. My insight into my inadequate responses will deepen, my conscience will become more sensitive in the light of these growing graces.

[11] *Catechism of the Catholic Church*, 1123.

The post Communion Prayer for the 27th. Sunday in Ordinary time says "Almighty God, let the Eucharist we share fill us with your life..." [12]. The Church wants to teach us reality so that we avoid abstractions; God wishes us to be assumed into His greatness, soul and body; He longs for my total conversion in every emotion, in my false ego, in my desire to dominate others. Pope Benedict XVI beautifully refers to this love in his encyclical. [13].This change includes how I meet God. The Eucharist invites surrendering every fibre of my being. In that great change of bread and wine into His Body and Blood, there is penetration into every region of my being, thoroughly to convert me so that I live more for His glory.

Through the Eucharist as the main channel of grace, the Holy Spirit sanctifies our souls. This is the principal sanctifying sacrament since it unites souls with Jesus. [14]. On 6th December 1273 while saying Mass, St. Thomas Aquinas saw that everything he had

---

[12] Cf. Latin: "Concéde nobis, omnípotens Deus, ut de percéptis sacraméntis inebriémur atque pascámur, quátenus in id quod súmimus transeámus."

[13] *Deus caritas est*, 9-10.

[14] Cf. Marie-Eugène de l'E.-J., *Je veux voir Dieu*, Édition du Carmel 1998, p. 1018.

written previously, even before the tabernacle, seemed to be like straw. He could write or dictate no more. Touching God, even in the light of faith, he now saw God really present. By comparison, everything else was valueless. In this change, I continue to see the same things but I see them very differently through the Holy Spirit's Eucharistic activity. The Eucharist gives me everything. St. Francis of Assisi saw the same Assisi so differently, even the entertainments. The Lord showed him true values. Everything took on a completely new value.

The spiritual life is a pathway. Each interior recess, winding corridor or passageway becomes amazingly transformed by the Eucharist. This change takes place in my thoughts and will. Christ wants to enlarge my soul's capacity so that my interior becomes more and more diverse. Illusions and mirages disappear more readily in this interior journey. I experience the emptiness of mirages which from a distance tempt and at close range poison with absurd bitterness. Francis saw the complete senselessness of his earlier life. He did not want to go back to spending empty days wasting his life; he was not afraid that his former companions would ridicule him. The Eucharist is mightily powerful for me too.

The Eucharist transfers me into Gospel times; I become a companion of Jesus as He walked this earth, instituting the Eucharist at the Last Supper, suffering painful betrayal and dying on the cross. In the Mass, these events take place in the light of the Lord's glory; thanks to the Mass, I am part of the Lord's Redemption with its inner radical changes.

The Eucharistic Sacrament gives hope and merciful healing; it is a very joyful way; the Lord comes into me and stays in me; at Mass He is on the altar; He stays with me in all my ups and downs; He carries me, working through my mysterious psychological processes so that He can help me to abandon myself to Him.

The Eucharist is the spiritual process by which God on the altar attempts to renew me very intensely. However poor my response, my interior responses are affected by events.

St. Margaret Mary Alacoque's convent life was pretty monotonous; yet the interior activity was intense. That life brought the rapid spread of devotion to Our Lord's Sacred Heart throughout the world; exterior activity is just the background to the reality which interiorly transforms us into new people living for God through Jesus Christ in the Holy Spirit. If I desire it "with all my heart, with all my soul and with all my mind" (cf. Mt 22,37), He will come to me as God the Most High, penetrating me by His sanctity, through and through; it is a sanctity which influences the whole Church.

Part II

CONCERN FOR SOULS

Faith is invisible; it is spiritual; its depth cannot be measured; it increases and flows invisibly. My feelings can delude me; I may think I am focused when I am praying without distractions; this may lead me to think I am contacting God when I am really concentrating on myself.

The Eucharist is the sacrament of faith. Our Faith can be measured by our concern for souls. This is a true indication of our growth in faith. If this is my concern as I am on my way to the Eucharist, I can be sure my faith is alive. This concern is at the heart of the Son of God's spiritual redemption- exactly that. God's care for my physical well-being is in view of my spiritual health. If I pray I shall find a job, I need to be mindful of faith. I need a job for a balanced outlook to develop spiritually and psychologically.

God gave the desert Chosen People supplies of manna and water in a way that never obscured their vital spiritual development. God overlooks no detail in His infinite concern for us. The Israelites in the desert, amazingly benefited from His Providence; wonders never ceased. Yet the Lord God constantly fought for their souls; He led them to share true human fulfilment of life in God; that is where we choose God's will over our own. Moses taught them about it. The Chosen People's hopes were rightly seen as always serving spiritual needs and concern for souls. Care for my soul brings me to share in the Eucharist. I would grasp it intensely if my spiritual concern were as deep as my care for my body. I need to get the balance right in order to remove obstacles on my way to God. I usually either worry too much about my body or forget it; my body is meant to help me.

God and soul point to the same reality. God unites with the soul to enliven my whole being. My body is to be my aid; God wants care for my body. It is vital to get this properly focused. Hurry and tension are signs that I am not correctly focused; frantic pursuit of pleasure, the joy of being in authority, possessiveness, too much emphasis on success, too much pursuit of power or money destroy our peace, make us ill, stressed and tense.

Faith gives peace; it helps us see that everything is transitory – health, job, family. Worry is so futile when I feel lonely and nobody wants me. Personal relationships, even the closest, are just for earthly life; souls are more important.

God seems to be far away, I do not see Him; people are near. "If anyone says, 'I love God', and hates his brother, he is a liar – writes St. John the Apostle – for he who does not love his brother whom he has seen, cannot love God whom he has not seen". (1 Jn 4,20). Concern for others' spirituality involves concern for my own spiritual development.

We usually have too little care for the soul; we live for the body; we often exaggerate the sadness of death. That is not the whole story; there is life beyond. I can only become more spiritual by pursuing sanctity.

TRUE LOVE FOR THE DEPARTED

The Eucharist as a sacrament, involves having an ever strengthening faith.[15] The strengthening process is not confined to Eucharistic celebration; it overflows into daily life. When I leave church and go about my life, Eucharistic grace goes with me. Whatever I do, wherever I go, with companions at home or at work, resting or eating, everything is different and related to God and his glory. "So, whether you eat or drink, or whatever you do, – says St. Paul – do all to the glory of God." (1 Cor 10,31)

When I pray for my mother at Mass and visit her grave, if my Communion is good and fruitful, my

---

[15] *Catechism of the Catholic Church*, 1123.

faith grows and improves how I view the reality of the cemetery visit.

Nearness of Christ has transformed me and changed my outlook. He who walked in Israel reigns in Eucharistic glory. By faith, in Communion, I 'touch' Him. As I go to the cemetery, my outlook is quite different. My worldly concerns which could cause me to be ill, have marvellously diminished through Eucharistic strengthening. In the light of my Eucharistic renewal, everything is renewed. So too is the way I look at visiting the cemetery.

There is more sense to my visiting the grave. My Eucharistic Lord transforms me so that I see the flowers I bring as a mere token of my faithful Eucharistic participation offered to the departed.

In the Eucharist, we pray for the deceased "Welcome into your kingdom our departed brothers and sisters." [16] We pray that our merciful God grants them a share in eternal light.

My love for my mother was really strong. I never forget her. Mothers are close to sons; they are ready to live for them completely in a great dedication. My mother lives on where there is no everyday hurry, race

[16] See: The Third Eucharistic Prayer.

against time, no concern about a job, no worry about myself. She sees everything differently. She lives in a different world whether in Heaven or in Purgatory. I come to visit her grave and to pray but she is no longer here.

Do I still love her? Loving is "looking outward together in the same direction" says Antoine de Saint Exupéry.[17] Love is creative, John Paul II tells us, a communion of persons, values and goals. So am I bonding with my mother? How can I if we live in different worlds with completely different values and goals? I may think I still love her. Yet I am so focused on worldly things; her focus is now so different. For her, the world I love no longer exists. Without common values, there is a void. Maybe mother sees my drama and desires as something to be avoided now that it is all so different for her. She now certainly wishes me to have a different focus.

To love means to have common values, desires, support and aims. To love my departed mother, I need to try to discover her world, move towards it, focus more like her. For love, it is essential to close that gap. In heaven, one is wrapped up in God; everything

[17] *Wind, Sand and Stars. Flight to Arras*, London 1987, p.141.

27

and everybody is involved in this focus. Mother cannot let this go; she sees how poor I am, so wrapped
up in worldly concerns, living in a world that is not
hers. She lives in a world of great light which leaves
me out in the gloomy shade.

If she is in Purgatory, she deeply regrets wasted
years as she goes through ardent purification. [18].
She is less and less interested in my sort of preoc-
cupations. Purgatorial purification radically alters the
focus. For sure, her changed vision inspires her to
regret the worldly focus she herself once shared. With
God's permission seeing what I am running after, she
must be stunned; my concerns only contribute to my
purgatorial suffering.

For sure she now wants my conversion. I need
this so that I can really communicate with and help
her. She will want communion with me. That is only
possible through my personal prayer permeating everyday life. This communion grows through detach-
ment from worldly illusions. When my Eucharistic
Redeemer converts me completely and abides in me,
I discover that it is not I who pray for my mother but
He. Then, with the appearance of the purest acts of

[18] Cf. *Catechism of the Catholic Church*, 1031.

28

love in me, she is brought to glory. Then I come to know that to love my mother is to long for union with her through Jesus.

DRAMA THE WORLD NEEDS TO DISCOVER

Mother Teresa was once with a young nun who was looking after a very sick person; this nun found it rather difficult. Mother Teresa asked her whether she had noticed how the priest at Mass touched Jesus under the species of bread. He did it with great adoration and love. She suggested the nun do the same when with the dying. She told her how she would meet Jesus in the sick and poor. Later the young nun came and said to Mother Teresa "Mother, thank you, for three hours I was touching Jesus". Now she is with Him.[19]

---

[19] Cf. *In the Silence of the Heart. Meditations by Mother Teresa of Calcutta,* compiled by Kathryn Spink, SPCK, London 1983, p.56.

It is a very telling story. Mother Teresa might ask me 'have you noticed how during Mass the priest with great adoration and love touches Eucharistic Jesus?' That helps me at home, in the street or any other place, to be spiritually caring. We all pine for God and need spiritual help. Many die from hunger for Him without realising it. Many live as if God does not exist. Day in, day out rushing around to do things so often pushes God out so that we hunger and die for lack of spiritual support.

Many die from hunger for God; yet actually it is God who dies in them as He has been cast out of their everyday lives. So many fall ill without even knowing why. They neither scream nor cry for help; these events are also opportunities. Mother Teresa is pointing to the greater spiritual care for Jesus in them. Like this young nun, I may also feel happy tending Jesus in them. This however might be difficult; for they either know nothing about their condition or have no time to meet me as they constantly hurry after worldly pursuits. Can I leave them sick and in need despite my realising that the Eucharist from which I have just come, continues? Like that priest touching the Eucharistic Jesus on the altar with great love and adoration, I am also to touch those who are needy. I owe them much for they prevent my excessively focusing on my selfish ego, helping me to unveil the power concealed in the Eucharist. This power is only limited by little faith; if I grow into God, it may change world events.

Part III

Every day prepares

In those moments when I am deeply open to Eucharistic faith, I begin to see into this amazing, puzzling, admirable miracle; I begin to see all other gifts as ephemeral; in isolation from Him, they are quite unworthy of my devotion. So I begin to long for the everlasting One who alone fulfils my yearnings. With these realisations, I pine all the more for this real transformation.

The Blessed Sacrament is connected with every moment of every day. The Eucharist is the opportunity for the change for which I long, turning even difficult events into something meaningful. Everything is meaningless which is not related to God and his Will. Yet my thoughts are rarely so faithful; God always wants me united with Him. He does not want me to miss great opportunities for grace.

On the way to union with God, every event becomes an act of worship. God's loving power helps us, sometimes even pushes us towards this 'liturgy'. "The true liturgical action is the deed of God, and for that very reason the liturgy of faith always reaches beyond the cult act into everyday life, which must itself become "liturgical", a service for the transformation of the world." writes Cardinal Joseph Ratzinger, today's Pope Benedict XVI[20].

I need to discover the world's complete dependence on God. Then I shall see that each event is an opportunity to prepare to share in the never-ending outpouring of redeeming Eucharistic graces. I need to appreciate God's pivotal, infinitely powerful position on the world's stage. His love inspires and oversees everything. Unless we are growing into an appreciation of this, Mass effectively means less. Without faith, I see nothing but an empty ritual. I need to start to see my everyday life in the light of faith.

---

[20] Joseph Cardinal Ratzinger, *The Spirit of the Liturgy*, 2000 Ignatius Press, San Francisco, p.175 [*Der Geist der Liturgie. Eine Einführung*, Freiburg i. Br. 2000.].

All my activity needs to be a worship of God. [21]; it needs to glorify God. Avoiding abstractions, St. Paul carefully teaches that everything should be dedicated to God. I glorify God by living for Him rather than for myself. When I try to live for His glory, my life may become an "earthly liturgy in everyday life". By an *earthly liturgy,* I live as St. Paul describes in his first letter to the Corinthians - *time is short, for the form of this world is passing away.* (cf. 1 Cor 7,29-31). As it becomes an act of divine worship, everything I do takes on wonderful new value. – *standing firmly on the ground I am fixing my eye on heaven,* said Pope Benedict in Cracow-Blonie, Poland. [22]. Unless I relate what I buy to God, it lacks real value and permanence; it is His money to be used in union with Him. Each true act of worship consists in my freely choosing His Will.

We need to deal with the world as though we are not dealing with it... in union with God, teaches the Apostle. The world is God's property. I need to live with this strong realisation; earthly liturgy fulfils God's will. When we live like that we experience the

[21] Cf. ibid.

[22] The homily during the Holy Mass in Cracow-Blonie, 28.05.2006.

joyous sense of timelessly fulfilling God's will in real Divine adoration: "Where God's will is done, there is heaven, there earth becomes heaven." [23].

"Israel left Egypt to serve God" writes Cardinal Ratzinger.[24] It was not just migration to the Promised Land. There was no sense in granting Israel new land, selfishly to grow rich in egocentric political or economic prosperity. God wanted Israel to have the Promised Land where He reigns. When He reigns, everything is rich through God-centeredness, freely chosen by us; that is real religious liturgy.

So human life needs just to be constant worship of God. St. Gertrude of Helfta vitally experienced the Lord's celebration of each Mass as if she were in heaven. That is because earthly liturgy belongs to the heavenly one.[25] Vatican II "attached great significance to the connection between earthly and heavenly liturgy" writes Cardinal Ratzinger, as

[23] Card. J. Ratzinger, op.cit., p. 176.

[24] Cf. ibid., p. 16-17.

[25] Cf. St. Gertrude of Helfta, *The Herald of Divine Love*, New York – Mahwah 1993, p. . The spiritual life of St. Gertrude called the Great, one of the greatest Christian mystics (1256 – circa 1301), remained, according to the Benedictine spirituality, in the direct connection with the liturgy. The Eucharist was the centre of the Saint's interior life. She comprehended the whole life (and not only the prayer) as one great cosmic liturgy taking place in heaven and on earth.

"thanks to Christ heaven was opened; participants in the liturgy are not only sharing the meeting of a certain circle. The radius of this circle reaches the Universe and the characteristic feature of the liturgy is that earth and heaven meet together. This is the greatness of Divine worship." [26] Both Mass and our earthly life need to reflect heavenly liturgy. Our aim should be constant, never-ending worship of God. I need to respond God's glory constantly flowing from the Eucharist into my life.

In moments of sadness, I need to remember not to concentrate on myself but to live *as though I were not mourning*, for *time has grown short*. If *the form of this world is passing away*, why be sad? God permits sad things in my life to inspire me to *fix my eye on heaven* so that what I do does not perish with time. I should worry less. I should not despair; there is no reason for this. If illusions pass – *the form of this world is passing away* – why worry? My egoism suffers because of attachments. Once I open myself to Eucharistic graces, in divine love I may see myself set free from illusions.

[26] Joseph Cardinal Ratzinger, *Foreword to the Polish edition*, in: *The Spirit of the Liturgy* (Polish: *Duch liturgii*), Poznań 2002, p. 6.

Rejoicing becomes worthy, St. Paul tells us if we do so *as though not rejoicing*. Rejoicing like that is deeper rejoicing by seeing everything in a more detached way. The Eucharist purifies every sorrow and joy; it transforms each of them into something indescribably better.

I need always to live thanking God for everything; I need to move towards the eternal *now;* every moment needs to be one which adores God. If I have good health, I need to rejoice with more humility and gratitude; then my rejoicing is more realistic – *the form of this world is passing away*; my health is also always ephemeral. In the Eucharist, things are transformed; so my rejoicing needs to be *as though not rejoicing*. The Eucharist gives birth to a new self within me. Only its works are eternal. My new self strives to rejoice *as though not rejoicing*. In my attitude to work too, I need Eucharistic transformation. The Benedictine maxim *ora et labora* should be understood in the sense that my work is a prayerful chord in an eternal symphony, performed for God.

FOR GOD'S GLORY?

Does what I do give glory to God? I sometimes wonder; faith answers. If I am anxious when I am interrupted, I am self-centred. Nothing happens without God's consent. It is He who interrupts me. Interruptions are His call for me to change what I am doing; interruptions have a deep meaning; my Eucharistic God is involved in them; Yet what really counts is His bringing me to the light of faith. This light unveils how I respond to His love which never stops caring for me. He simply longs to free me from my attachments.

Perhaps that is why there are certain turning points in my life. God wants to rescue me from my self-centredness; He comes to my rescue. His call to me to change what I am doing is full of meaning. I need to adjust my plans in the light of Eucharistic faith; then my sadness turns into Eucharistic joy.

I can see Him in each event. I may need to leave what I am doing to help somebody. He always wants to save me from myself. My personal peace increases as I follow His Will. He surprises me with His interruptions which change my plans to bring me to be more open to His Eucharistic presence. It helps to be on the lookout to meet Him by allowing His redemptive, Eucharistic activity to have more influence in my conscience. Only then will I be able to be open to worship our hidden Eucharistic God.

When I am tired and weary, prone to impatience, when everything seems to be a burden, I have opportunities to begin to see if my activity is Eucharistic. These are great opportunities to call for the Holy Spirit to descend into me and worship God as St. Thérèse of Lisieux wonderfully teaches in her Little Way. St. Therese depicts Jesus at the top of a flight of stairs. A small child, trying to climb up to reach Him, constantly slides down the stairs. With even greater determination, he keeps trying again, staring at the face of Jesus in a way that spells out: *I need*

You. This goes on until Jesus comes down and takes him into His arms. Now they are inseparable. [27].

If I seem to have no time when I long to be with our hidden God in Eucharistic adoration, He invites me to adore Him in my activities, avoiding tendencies to be sad or agitated. He is also near me all the time when I am worrying about my poor prayer. I need to avoid concentrating on myself. Each activity is an opportunity for His grace and glory. Pope John Paul II encourages me to stay before Jesus in the tabernacle so that I *sense His heartbeat*. [28]. Our Eucharistic Lord also invites me to adore Him in what I am doing, so that here too I can feel God's heartbeat. I need to believe I can adore Him in this way. That should be my one and only goal; frustration vanishes when I see things like this.

Whatever I am doing, I only have this present moment to adore Him in acts of faith, hope and love. In this way, life becomes really worthwhile; yet at any time, He may call me for great eternal life with Him. It is my faith that defines the value of what He

---

[27] Cf. *Procès de béatification et canonisation de sainte Thérèse de l'Enfant-Jésus et de la Sainte-Face*, Roma 1973, p. 488.

[28] Cf. The Apostolic Letter *Mane nobiscum Domine*, 18.

reveals to me in each event so that I need Him all the more. His extraordinary nearness prompts me to share it with others.

EUCHARISTIC LOVE GIVES BIRTH TO SAINTS

The Eucharist is the Sacrament of love; It is an extraordinary sacrament of extraordinary love. Our once visible Jesus now wants to give us His invisible sacramental presence. He mysteriously remains very close to us in outstanding, incomprehensible love. Pope John Paul II confirms that Jesus waits for me in this Sacrament of love. [29]; there is nothing I need more. I need faith to believe it; I need an ever deepening faith.

Our belief in the gloriously resurrected One, present in this mysterious Sacrament is nowhere near deep enough. He is constantly accessible. In Palestine He

---

[29] Cf. The Apostolic Letter *Dominicae cenae*, 3.

was in one place at a time. Crowds simply forgot how tired they were; they just wanted to be near Him. Now we can be near Him everywhere in the world in countless tabernacles and Masses. He who died for us, ceaselessly loves us in His Eucharistic Presence. Since He paid the highest price to make us whole by saving us, His friendship is unquestionable.

The Eucharist takes place *ex opere operato*: i.e. It is caused just by the words which are spoken.[30] The same Eucharistic Presence continues to be really present in every church after the Consecration. I do not appreciate this nearly enough. I do not have anything like a proper recognition of this extraordinary, incomprehensible gift. It is a gift greater than His physical Presence in Palestine.

I need the impact of our Eucharistic Lord; I need to be more open to Him; I need to believe in this Sacrament of love; He stays because He loves to be with me. Frequent contact with Him in this Sacrament affects me enormously. It is similar to when our Saviour walked in the Holy Land; everyone had the choice to accept, reject or simply ignore Him. People who met great saints like St. Jean-Marie Vianney or

[30] *Catechism of the Catholic Church*, 1128.

St. Pio of Pietrelcina, were often deeply transformed, even though gradually.

"For I fear Jesus passing by" [31] St. Augustine said. It is the same with our Eucharistic Lord. Irrespective of how we respond, He is really present; He is hidden from our senses; He is in our minds if we are focused in the light of faith. Every Mass offers us choice; we receive grace; moreover we are in touch with the divine incarnate Source of grace itself. He stays so near us in His glory, surrounded by invisible hosts of Angels. Human presences somehow affect us; yet we are much more prone to be affected by the Divine Presence. Goodness is by nature diffusive of itself; the world wide supernatural Eucharistic goodness on altars and in tabernacles has infinite impact. Love always communicates itself even though it can be resisted. Yet This One needs to be my One and only Master and Love.

Attending Mass with careful attention gives me valuable opportunities for extraordinary graces. Any inadequacies in my attitude can impede them. "If I had not come and spoken to them, they would not have sinned; but now they have no excuse for their

[31] St. Augustine, *Sermones*, LXXXVIII, 13.

sin" (Jn 15,22). If I go to Mass just out of habit, I can increase my Purgatory. Yet I also have great opportunity to discover this Only Love for which I deeply pine.

In every Eucharist, the Lord assures me of His love. I should not ignore this; it is too important. I must not reject God. If the power of grace wins me over, I should try to be with Him more and more; I can spend hours and hours before the tabernacle, remaining in His sanctifying love and power. It will draw me to desire much more life with Him; I need to open myself to this great challenge.

It is faith's great mystery. Jesus fell in love with me. He proves it in these Eucharistic meetings, the extraordinary source of my completeness in sanctity. When I respond by falling in love with this sacramental One, my love will be on the way to that wholeness called sanctity. It involves growth in loving thanks through faith and hope. The Eucharist is the normal and easiest way to holiness. By the Eucharist, God loves constantly; by the Eucharist He is available with His infinite power and love.

It is by faith that I relate to Eucharistic Love. Yet this development is a challenging battle.[32] I am either

[32] Cf. *Catechism of the Catholic Church*, 2725.

invisibly approaching Him or retreating. It is most important to remember that I should not analyse or focus on it. Prayer is a struggle; my sharing in the Eucharist is consequently also a struggle. I need to allow myself to be receptive to the power of the Holy Spirit seeking to transform my resistance by the flame of Its Love. That is the challenge; to make progress, I need a big miracle. God's glory will then spiritually enter my life. This glory inflames me once I allow the Holy Spirit to sanctify me.

Eucharistic love gives birth to saints. Sanctity cannot be egocentric; it is for the growth of the Lord's Mystical Body; it is the spiritual fruit of union with Christ in love. "Christ and the Church are just one thing"[33] says St. Joan of Arc. The Eucharist gives birth to that wholeness in self-forgetfulness so that the Lord's Mystical Body is built up. As a result, more Saints appear. I need to love the Church along with that sign of unity, St. Peter's successor because the Lord especially marked him out by praying to strengthen his faith (cf. Lk 22:31-32). I am to become

---

[33] A reply of St. Joan of Arc to her judges sums up the faith of the holy doctors and the good sense of the believer: "About Jesus Christ and the Church, I simply know they're just one thing, and we shouldn't complicate the matter." - *Catechism of the Catholic Church*, 795.

so small that the Holy Spirit, Father of the small and poor can bring me to the maturity of sanctity; I need to become an instrument for Him to transform the face of the earth.

LIFE AS LITURGY

Ineed to be at Mass viewing my life as a mysterious divine tapestry seen upside down, distorted and unintelligible. *I do not know what You are weaving, Lord but I know You love me. I return everything to You; I do not understand it either in this sacramental liturgy or in the liturgy of my life.*

The Eucharist is a source of power, light and peace. Insecure everyday feelings make me ready for Divine rescue. Sacramental liturgy and God's service in everyday life are interconnected; they also interact. My puzzling sense of loss is an enormous opportunity for renewal in Eucharistic love.

When I do not understand things, I worry more about tomorrow; changes around me seem to be outpacing my ability to cope; I experience some instability in myself and the family, the community and at work; changes in the weather get me down; unknown changes in nature, gradual climate changes and floods worry me because I am no longer in control of events. In these events, God takes away my secure, comfortable thrones.

It is all like a storm I cannot control. It is like that storm on the Sea of Galilee which the Apostles, experienced fishermen, could not control. Yet all this is great opportunity to be open to the Eucharist. These events show me that we human beings are not in control, that we need more faith to be in touch with the One Reality present on the altar who determines events in the macro and micro world. It is only by faith that I can be open to God's extraordinary Eucharistic presence. These anxieties are my opportunities to grow in faith. In such difficult moments God speaks: *This is your trial of faith; this is your Galilean storm.*

We recall Jesus in one of several fishing boats on the Sea of Galilee. The Apostles were certain they would reach the shore; everything seemed normal. Suddenly their thought patterns were dashed; huge waves crashed onto the ship's deck; the boat began to sink. They were struck with terror; they were in danger of death; those fishermen lost their nerve; things got out of control; even the experienced sons of Zebedee, James and John were quite lost as they battled against the elements.

I now see more clearly that it is not at all a good thing to know or understand so much. I can see more clearly the value of a puzzling tapestry. Eucharistic Jesus longs not to be pushed out of my life. He pines to be at the helm of my boat. My Christian vocation is to choose Him as the mainstay of my life. We learn from such things as this event on the Sea of Galilee; the Apostles needed to grow into deeper faith. Growth in faith is challenging and life long. It is clear that the Apostles were not deeply convinced until the Holy Spirit took hold of them at Pentecost. From the choice of the Apostles and their formation, there are important lessons for us to learn. These events in that storm on the Galilean Sea are very valuable. "What sort of man is this, that even winds and sea obey him?" (Mt 8,27). That was the question. The Apostles got to know the Master much more. We can presume that was the only purpose of the Galilean storm. The Apostles had so much to learn about faith in His power. They still lacked understanding; frightened and full of amazement, they ask again and again: "Who is he?"

I need to admit I do not know or understand the Eucharist where the same Jesus who silenced the storm raging on the Sea of Galilee, is present. Throughout my whole life I need to learn more about the Lord who calls me to faith. He wants me to find Him in the Eucharist. Through life's storms, He is able to bring radical changes into my faith; I can learn to know Him much more by the experience of His mighty power and love. I shall have similar fears as He draws me to believe in His saving grace. For sure, I shall also cry out: "Lord, do You not care if I perish?!" Without such meaningful storms, I cannot grow into the depths of God's amazingly powerful love.

Perhaps I still have to choose Jesus. Maybe I am still so attached to outward religious practices and duties that I do no see them as barriers to the inner meeting with our Eucharistic God. Perhaps I do not really meet Him in this extraordinary liturgy at the altar. Maybe my participation in the Mass is still pretty ritualistic and habitual; maybe I do not have a very deep understanding of this amazing radical saving love He is offering me.

When I see these overpowering trials of faith, it is helpful to remember Our Lady's outstanding faith. The Apostles were full of worries about their future as they waited in the Cenacle. Mary who stayed awake with them in prayer " taught perseverance in the faith" – writes Pope Benedict XVI – "... she teaches us how to pray. Mary shows us how to open our minds and our hearts to the power of the Holy Spirit, who comes to us in order to be brought to the whole world. ... we need a moment of silence and recollection to place ourselves in her school, so that she may teach us how to live by faith, how to grow in faith, how to remain in contact with the mystery of God in the ordinary, everyday events of our lives."[34].

The *Catechism* teaches that prayer is "being in the presence of the thrice-holy God and in communion with Him." [35]. In sending me storms, He forces me

[34] Benedict XVI, *Address by the Holy Father, Encounter with Men and Women Religious, Seminarians and Representatives of Ecclesial Movements,* Częstochowa, 26 May 2006, *www.vatican.va/holy_father/benedict_xvi/ speeches/2006/may/index_en.htm*

[35] *Catechism of the Catholic Church,* 2565.

to choose Him in constant prayer. I need to cry out or I shall perish. God wants me always to seek Him like the persistent widow with the unjust judge; we need incessant prayer. (cf. Lk 18,1-8) Our Eucharistic God is waiting for me; He wants me always to need Him; He wants me to find my necessary wholeness by constant prayer in communion with our hidden Eucharist God.

Part IV

Tough challenge to find freedom

Every Mass mysteriously leads me towards the Lord's death and resurrection. By the Eucharist, I am always led to move from the transitory to the permanent. Our Eucharistic God wants to free me from passing possessive attachments to live in His interior grace. He wants me to move away from illusions towards reality.

As God created it, the world is good. Yet when I am possessive or avaricious, my view of it is muddled. When I want to conquer people for myself and fail, I get sad that I am not accepted; I can become a sort of slave. I lose my ability to support others. So once again I am overcome with sadness. Our Eucharistic

God longs to free me from these disturbances so He can love me very deeply without possessiveness and manipulation. He wants to free me from the unrest arising from frequently disordered emotions.

St. John of the Cross teaches freedom from attachments. He sheds extremely vital light. It is only by loss of attachments that I can find the freedom to love our Eucharistic Lord. In a nutshell, interior life is an increasing freedom for God's love and my choice to receive it. When far away from Him, I undermine His saving death. My possessive attachments to people and things make me revolve around myself instead of revolving around Him. I make Him too small in my life. I still seek my own greatness, my imaginary thrones. My desire to possess and control are selfish desires to promote my own glory. They obscure and impede the transmission of real Eucharistic love. The redemptive action of the Eucharist brings freedom from possessive attachments in my everyday life. For this freedom I pray in every Mass awaiting the fulfilment of His promise 'my peace I give you'. I need to pray for this peaceful freedom; it protects me from destructive, diverting confusions; these push Eucharistic graces out of my life.

I need to be at Mass with the humble attitude of a returning prodigal. I need to be there with a deeply repentant heart. I need to make big efforts to achieve this attitude just like the Prodigal Son. Pope John Paul II affirms that we are all prodigal.[36]. This is the way I need to be present at Mass; like the Prodigal Son, I need to be free from illusions of personal greatness and self-sufficiency, managing quite well without the Father. Freed from these illusions and repentant, I can become more open to God's Eucharistic grace.

God wants all the events in my life to be open to His loving grace. That is why there is the Eucharist; everything needs to be related to this redemptive activity. God deeply cherishes my sanctification and salvation. With enormous persuasion, my loving God invites me to respond. By His outstanding love, He longs for everything in the visible and invisible world to assist my relationships to be more loving. He wants to free that boat stuck in the mud; He may even permit the flood to rise and push my boat towards the main current. By this He improves my insights into His actions. He wants to motivate prodigal sons and daughters to return to redemptive Eucharist. He

[36] *Reconciliatio et paenitentia*, 5.

wants to lead me to true loving relationships; He has the answer to life's puzzling failures by false love and attachments.

Through many experiences and disappointments, I am drawn towards Him who never disappoints; I surely need this Rock of support; without It, all is fragile. I need to be as sure of unfailing loving power coming from Jesus in the Eucharist as I am of the world's fragility.

Our divine Lord uniquely improves my thoughts; without His presence and works, everything is empty. I need deeply to fill myself with Him. He wants me to mature in His love so that I focus on what is more meaningful. I need to avoid the superficial. So He calls me to the Eucharist where He, the real controller of world events, is really present.

The Eucharist, sacrament of faith not only pre-supposes our faith but feeds it too. The *Constitution on the Sacred Liturgy* [37] teaches that events in my life should open me to a grace filled faith. I need to share in God's vision. I need to move from fragility to stability since in God's eyes the world is not frag-ile; it is stable. I need to improve my thinking about

[37] *Constitution on the Sacred Liturgy, 59.*

earthquakes and volcanoes; in reality, I need to learn that I am usually less threatened by these than I am by walking on some of those insecure paving stones. My attitude towards these worrying events needs to develop in the light of faith.

It takes a long time to learn these things. It is a lifelong challenging struggle to experience the freedom of seeing rough lava hardening after a volcanic eruption with a little of the equanimity one views our city streets. The Apostles only learned slowly. There was no fire, smoke or lava on the Sea of Galilee but there was a powerful storm, shaking the boat so much that everything trembled before their eyes. It was exactly by such trials that the Twelve grew in faithful discipleship. Jesus rebuked them for a lack of faith. Jesus even slept for a while when the storm was in progress. From this, He gave them a lesson in belief.

Like the Twelve, I need constantly to grow in faith, more fully to participate in the reality of the Eucharist. This is my challenge; like the Apostles, I need to learn to share in this extraordinary Eucharistic sacrificial light. By this I shall find more than adequate love and support to inspire me to share the Good News even to the ends of the earth. I need

this Eucharistic love so much. I may not realise that
this is my basic need. I am created for happiness.
I can only find it in Him, my constant, redemptive,
Eucharistic God Who gives Himself for me. This is
the Sacrament-Sacrifice.[38]. He is always waiting for
me at the altar and in the tabernacle. It is the Sacrament of Presence. He pines to fill me with happiness
and love. He longs for me to remove the obstacles
so that I can receive the extraordinary grace of His
presence on earth. This is a Sacrament-Communion.
He wants me to take up this tough challenge so that
I find some heavenly freedom on earth. He longs for
me to share this glory – right now. Now is the time
He wants to give Himself to me. He wants me to
permit it – right now.

---

[38] „With all the greater reason, then, it is not permissible for us, in thought,
life or action, – emphasizes John Paul II – to take away from this truly
most holy Sacrament its full magnitude and its essential meaning. It is at
one and the same time a Sacrifice-Sacrament, a Communion-Sacrament,
and a Presence-Sacrament" – *Redemptor hominis*, 20.

Emptiness God longs
TO FILL

"May He make us an everlasting gift to You"
we read in the third Eucharistic Prayer.
We pray to become an eternal gift to the Father; the
whole of heaven ceaselessly prays that I respond with
complete dedication to Him so that He can completely
give Himself to me.

It is not easy for me to sacrifice myself to God. I
learn gradually; all my life I need to learn that He is
so near that I am never alone. I am never surrounded
by emptiness. When it is silent and I feel empty, it
is an illusion. He can fill my heart; only He can do
this; only He can give me the grace of sacrificing
myself to the Father completely; my emptiness can

lead me to the fullness discovered through faith. God created the emptiness in which I seem to drown; only He uncovers the truth that actually I always live in emptiness. For a while someone may fill my heart with the illusion that I am not empty. Sooner or later the reality dawns.

By His grace God draws me to learn that my emptiness only results from lack of external stimuli. When noise and trivialities cease, I experience silence. This is the opportunity for faith to be born in me. Liberation from noise is God's gift. God can now fill me with His joyous presence instead of the frequent distraction of radio and TV. Through my emptiness He asks my consent to accept it.My emptiness, seen in faith, is paradoxically full. The third Eucharistic Prayer mentions the presence of Our Lady, saints and angels. They never stop praying for me, sharing God's wonderful concern for me. They long for me to stop running after earthly noisy distractions; they long for me to be full of this spiritual joy when I see my emptiness always full of His outstanding presence.

I need gradually to learn the reality of faith. Real love comes from angels and our heavenly neighbours.

Their continual liturgy is praise of God which necessarily involves unceasing prayerful concern for me. They long for me to share my life with the Lord. This is their constant concern; they are always intervening with the prayer God longs to be offered; they pray that I respond with the complete gift of myself. He pines for me who thinks I am empty and abandoned. If I deeply open myself in the grace of faith, I can discover that this emptiness is God's gift to me. It helps me to find Him in the presence of the saintly and angelic forces which are always there with Him. As I struggle with my emptiness, I am frequently unaware that God is trying to move closer to me. When I realise this, by faith I can discover the reality of His love present on the altar. He is constantly longing to redeem me. I need to believe this. My faith tells me that those prayers and gestures at Mass are far from being empty rites.

My worldly concerns and activities obscure God's closeness to me in this greatest event in the world. I need this silent emptiness to feed me with Eucharistic love. I must not miss this vital daily influence. I can only absorb God's Eucharistic presence by a silent heart which is not driven by passions. This makes room for the Invisible One. Empty silence makes room for the Eucharist to transform me as *eternal gift* to the Father; Mass is redemption-sanctification. "Make us an everlasting gift to You" is the request. The entire Mystical Body, Christ and the members long for my wholeness in what we call sanctity. "Make us an everlasting gift to You" reminds me to learn to live by the extraordinary prayer of the Blessed Charles de Foucauld: *Live as if I were to die today.*[39]. That was his daily maxim. If I live like this, all problems disappear; nothing needs to be completed. Nothing improves my focus more than to think I have only a few hours before I die.

This prayer, composed by Blessed Charles in Algeria can help me. By faith I learn not to be afraid to be empty; I learn to strive for it as my meeting point with God. He is ceaselessly preparing to meet me; Mass tells me of His care for me. Our Lady, the heavenly hosts of Apostles, Martyrs and Saints are praying for me; they pray for my faith and for the gift of prayer which quietens my heart. That is how it was

---

[39] In Béni Abbès, in 1903, Charles de Foucauld writes: *Vivre aujourd'hui comme si je serais mourir ce soir martyr. Live as if I were to die a martyr today.* Jean-Jacques Antier, *Charles de Foucauld*, 1999 Ignatius Press, San Francisco, p.322.

with Blessed Charles. God has no greater desire than to meet me. He gives me everything. Without Him, I am nothing. I need the grace of emptiness. Blessed Charles de Foucauld helps me. With that prayer of his, I will surely get my priorities right; it helps me see that so many of my daily concerns are quite futile.

As my earthly concerns fall into obscurity, You God remain, present in the Eucharist. You who love me infinitely, lead me to Yourself. You are always waiting for me to be full of faith in Your merciful love, waiting for me to cry out with Thomas the Apostle: My Lord and my God. You long to take me to Yourself, to dry every tear from my eyes, to remove every torment from my heart. You are everything for me; You want me to discover this through faith. You want me to discover that You, Eucharistic Jesus, daily publish Your Sacrifice as the expression and proof of incomprehensible love for me. I need to believe that this is the love which some day will lead me to be united with You in glory.

FATHER, I ADORE YOU...

The best book on the Eucharist is the Eucharist Itself. One cannot fully understand mysteries; one cannot fully understand this Most Holy Sacrament. The Eucharistic presence is incomparably unique. It is sacramental; It endures in time and yet It is timeless; thanks to the Species, It is spatial yet surpasses space. A difficulty for us is that what is unseen is more real than what is seen. Access to our Eucharistic God is only by faith. So Mass is rather like a test of faith. We remember the great resistance Our Lord met in Capernaum. He spoke of forthcoming Eucharist; He said He is the living Bread and Its reality, "He who eats my flesh and drinks my blood abides in me, and I in him" (Jn 6,56). The Eucharist is the measure of my faith now just as it was for the people of Capernaum. Under pressure, He did not alter His firm stance. Drinking blood was forbidden; "Whoever eats any blood, that person shall be cut off from his people" (Lev 7,27). Despite this, He kept exactly to His words; the Eucharist measures my faith in Him.Faith is clinging to His words and even more to Him who is Love Itself. His words, especially these strong ones, remain firm; the Eucharist is giving Himself for us.

Mass should inspire me to faith in His redeeming Sacrifice. My spiritual growth depends on clinging to Him through love as this is the highest form of coming to know Him.

My individual and personal growth into Eucharistic adoration and love during and apart from Mass, is the way I contribute to the building up of the Mystical Body. I also need the intimacy of being alone with Him. Sometimes graces are only given in those moments. At one time, many people left for the desert in the search of solitude. They sought to deepen their contact with the Almighty. I can constantly adore my Eucharistic God in the tabernacle. Here I find Love Itself; I hope this outstanding nearness leads me to be in love with Him.

"Here, once again, I only wish to underline", says Benedict XVI, "adoration of the Risen Lord, present in the Eucharist with flesh and blood, with body and soul, with divinity and humanity. ... In the period of liturgical reform, Mass and Adoration outside of Mass were often seen as in opposition to one another; it was thought that the Eucharistic Bread had not been given to us to be adored but to be eaten; a widespread objection claimed this at that time. The experience of the prayer of the Church has already shown how nonsensical this antithesis was. Augustine had formerly said: "...No one should eat this flesh without first adoring it;... we should sin were we not to adore it". Indeed, we do not merely receive something in the Eucharist. It is a meeting and union of persons; the Person, however, who comes to meet us and desires to unite himself to us is the Son of God. Such union can only be brought about by means of adoration. Receiving the Eucharist means adoring the One whom we receive. We become one with Him precisely and only in this way. The development of Eucharistic adoration, as it took shape during the Middle Ages, was the most consistent consequence of the Eucharistic mystery itself: only in adoration can profound and true acceptance develop."[40].

Fruitful reception of the Eucharist needs me to be humble and loving through faith. Paradoxically, I mature in understanding this extraordinary Eucharistic mystery and find the love involved, the more I develop in childlike faith. Amazingly, our Saviour bends in admiration towards those who are helpless and small before Him: "I give You Praise, Lord of heaven and earth, for although you have hidden these things from the wise and the learned you have revealed them to the childlike" (Lk 10,21).

My fruitful relationship with the Eucharist is dependent on my becoming small before God so that He can reveal the mystery of His presence under the species of bread and wine. This mystery contains the hidden seeds of my sanctification. I need to grow into a greater awareness of my finiteness before Infinite Eucharistic Presence. That is the only way Jesus can communicate and reveal to me the depths of His unfathomable love. My faith appeals to God; He turns to me insofar as I am spiritually small. Poverty of

[40] *Address of His Holiness Benedict XVI to the Roman Curia offering them his Christmas greetings*, 22.12.2005.

spirit leads me to be more truly finite so that I may mature in the loving treasure our infinite Eucharistic Saviour longs to share with me.

A WOMAN OF THE EUCHARIST

"In the Eucharist, Christ gives us the very body which he gave up for us on the cross, the very blood which he poured out..."[41]. Mary was the first to walk on the Eucharistic threshold. Thanks to her *fiat,* she conceived the Son who meets us in the Blessed Sacrament. She suffered social disapproval through her divinely arranged pregnancy before St. Joseph, on angelic advice, married her. We do not know the duration of these sufferings. Possibly, suspicion continued even when she went to live in St. John's home; she suffered a lot from her family who thought Jesus was out of his mind... (cf. Mk 3,20f).

[41] *Catechism of the Catholic Church,* 1365.

The Immaculate One lived among sinners. She needed growing faith to live with everyday difficulties. Many misunderstandings also demanded even more faith from her. The disappearance of Jesus when He was twelve, to be found later in the temple, is just one instance of her anxieties. Our Lady was frequently puzzled by Her Son's insights. She could never have understood the anxieties involved in God's mysterious earthly life before that all revealing descent of the Holy Spirit. God asked more from Mary than He asked from Abraham. It was always challenging not only as she stood at the foot of the cross but also in daily living. She needed much faith in Jesus' greatness to sustain her as she watched her Child's helplessness. Through continual trials of faith, she became deeply rooted in His redemptive work.

Jesus could leave us His Body and Blood because they had been received from Mary. "The body given up for us and made present under sacramental signs was the same body which she had conceived in her womb! For Mary, receiving the Eucharist, must have somehow meant welcoming once more into her womb that heart which had beat in unison with hers."[42].

[42] John Paul II, *Ecclesia de Eucharistia*, 56.

Ave, verum Corpus natum de Maria Virgine! – Hail, true Body, truly born Of the Virgin Mary mild![43] She "has given to the Lord the innocent Body and the most precious Blood that we receive at the altar. *Ave, verum Corpus*, the true Body, conceived by the Holy Spirit, carried in the womb with great love. ... This Body and Blood, present after the Consecration and sacrificed to the Father, have become the communion of love for all, strengthening us in unity by the Holy Spirit, to build the Church. ... Each Mass introduces us into the closest communion with Her, the Mother whose sacrifice manifests itself in the words of consecration."[44].

Falling in love with our Eucharistic God inspires us to fall in love with her who, by God's design, is so intimately involved. There would be no Eucharist if it were not for Mary.

We adore and receive the Blessed Sacrament given us through Mary's uniquely close co-operation. The Lourdes' Corpus Christi procession starts at the Grotto of Massabielle to emphasize that Mary gave us

---

[43] The beginning of the Eucharistic hymn dating from the 14th century and attributed to Pope Innocent VI (1282-1362).

[44] John Paul II, *The Angelus*, 05.06.1983.

Eucharistic Jesus who wants to give us everything. Jesus no longer walks this earth; we live in "the age of the Church."[45]. I do not have to look for the historical Jesus. He is here in the Eucharistic Presence. The hymn *Ave verum* underlines it. Once He was with people of Palestine; now He continues his Presence sacramentally.

This is something much more than His life in history. Through faith in the Eucharist, I can 'touch' Him, 'kiss' His feet just like the adulterous woman. He can stay with me as He stayed with Martha in Bethany. I can listen to Him as Mary listened to Him, sitting at His feet. On the altar, it is the same Jesus whose feet Mary Magdalene anointed with oil and wiped with her hair. It is the same Jesus who seeks me, gives me Himself so that I am never without Him. Through faith, I can help Him carry the Cross; at Mass He longs to find me. He arranged for this to happen in union with Mary. His Body was taken from hers. She never leaves Him who is always present in the Eucharist. God, our Emmanuel is only *with us through her.*

[45] Cf. *Catechism of the Catholic Church*, 1076.

I can only understand the Eucharist if I understand the Incarnation. [46]. The Eucharist is connected with the Lord's comings, firstly in that Nazareth Incarnation, secondly on the Eucharistic altar, thirdly in glory on the last day. The Eucharist is temporal, given to me to go through the night before the Lord's day, full of glory. Pope John Paul II describes Mary's extraordinary involvement in the Mass: "...in addition to her sharing in the Eucharistic banquet, there is an indirect picture of Mary's relationship with the Eucharist beginning with her interior disposition. *Mary is a "woman of the Eucharist" in her whole life.* The Church, which looks to Mary as a model, is also called to imitate her in her relationship with this most holy mystery."[47].

Pope John Paul II shows Mary as "the Eucharistic woman". He writes "In a certain sense Mary lived her *Eucharistic faith* even before the institution of the Eucharist, by the very fact that *she offered her virginal womb for the Incarnation of God's Word.* The Eucharist, while commemorating the Passion and Resurrection, is also in continuity with the Incarna-

---

[46] Cf. St. Irenaeus, *Adversus haereses*, V, 2,3.

[47] *Ecclesia de Eucharistia*, 53.

tion. At the Annunciation, Mary conceived the Son of God in the physical reality of His body and blood, thus anticipating within herself what to some degree happens sacramentally in every believer who receives, under the signs of bread and wine, the Lord's body and blood."[48].

We need to worship her and ask her to teach us how to anticipate the Church's Eucharistic faith."When, at the Visitation, she bore in her womb the Word made flesh, she became in some way a 'tabernacle' – the first 'tabernacle' in history – in which the Son of God, still invisible to our human gaze, allowed Himself to be adored by Elizabeth, radiating His light as it were through the eyes and the voice of Mary."[49]. "And is not the enraptured gaze of Mary, as she contemplated the face of the newborn Christ and cradled him in her arms that unparalleled model of love which should inspire us every time we receive Eucharistic communion?"[50]. Pope John Paul encourages me to follow St. John by taking Mary *to myself,* to share her dispositions, opening myself to more grace by faith

[48] Ibid., 55.
[49] Ibid.
[50] Ibid.

84

in the Lord: "What must Mary have felt as she heard from the mouth of Peter, John, James and the other Apostles the words spoken at the Last Supper: "This is my body which is given for you" (*Lk* 22:19)?"[51].

"The body given up for us and made present under sacramental signs – writes the Pope – was the same body which she had conceived in her womb! For Mary, receiving the Eucharist must have somehow meant welcoming once more into her womb that heart which had beat in unison with hers and reliving what she had experienced at the foot of the Cross. ... It means accepting – like John – the one who is given to us anew as our Mother. ... The *Magnificat* expresses Mary's spirituality, and there is nothing greater than this spirituality for helping us to experience the mystery of the Eucharist."[52].

Pope John Paul II emphasises: "The Church has received the Eucharist from Christ her Lord not as one gift – however precious – among so many others, but as *the gift par excellence*, for it is the gift of Himself, of His person in His sacred humanity, as well as the

---

[51] Ibid., 56.
[52] Ibid., 56-58.

gift of His saving work..."[53]. Pope John Paul II reveals His Eucharistic love, "The *Year of the Eucharist* has its source in the amazement with which the Church contemplates this great Mystery. It is an amazement which I myself constantly experience..."[54].

I stand and knock. I knock so you will open for Me. Then if you wish, I will give you to My Mother. She gave Me Body and Blood, conceived by the Holy Spirit, borne in Her womb with extraordinary love, present on the altar so It becomes the communion of love for all. You are in the same situation as She is. She received Me into Herself, after offering Me Herself with body and soul. Ask Her, who once received Me into Her body, to assist you now to receive Me to make your heart an extraordinary tabernacle, a tabernacle of continuous adoration.

---

[53] Ibid., 11.
[54] John Paul II, *Mane nobiscum Domine*, 29.

The graces inspiring my books of Eucharistic meditations, are closely connected with personally meeting St. Pio in San Giovanni Rotondo, Southern Italy. This meeting took place two years before his death; the highlight was his Mass. Convinced of his holiness, I waited for Mass which started at 4am. I was only a few metres from him.

I cannot forget the face of one who SAW. He was talking silently with SOMEONE on the altar. I have no doubt that Padre Pio was talking with a LIVING PERSON.

The Author